CONTENTS

Dedication

To my daughters who continue to inspire me to be a better father, grandfather, and man. To my wife, thank you for helping me achieve what success I have had with all three.

To my father who lost his battle with Covid-19 but won the battle of life.

Acknowledgments

To Barry Lyons, thank you for all your great work editing this project.

Thank you to my Ecana brothers and all those who took time for conversation to help develop and challenge my ideas. You were instrumental in broadening my perspective on topics that both directly and indirectly influenced the writing of this book.

1. Fear, Greed, Ignorance

I wrote this book while having a very uneasy feeling that with the current trajectory of our conversations, we will sacrifice another generation of African American children due to fear, greed, and ignorance. What fuels this unease is a sense that there is an acute lack of understanding of what really matters, of what will really make a difference. We have a headline mentality, a collection of one-liners without the depth to bring meaningful, measurable, and consequential change.

I just read an article written by Christina Wyman for the *Detroit Free Press* titled "Dear White People: Stop Confessing to White Privilege. Start Acting To End It." After reading it, I concluded that we have disagreements, but on the headline, we agree: we need to start acting.

Forget about the confessions of White privilege; this is not about White people. It is about eliminating Black disadvantage.

The focus for this book is not to dwell on platitudes and headlines that do little to address the racial divide. The purpose of this book is to focus on what matters. Education, safe housing, jobs (capital), a balanced criminal justice system, and a culture that values the family and all Black lives: fixing those problems will help save the next generation of African American children. Sound bites and trendy themes will not.

All the talk about racism, White privilege, money, and a host of other *insightful inaction* will do little to move things forward and break down current day African American barriers. Eliminating Black disadvantage will. What will help is addressing:

Fear.

The elimination of fear, from within both the Black and White communities who know better but are afraid to voice their feelings that this is not all about racism and money. Over the past three years I have talked to a number of Black leaders concerning what feeds the gap between White and Black youth. Racism unto itself was not at the top of the list. Items that headed the list included substandard education, unsafe housing, lack of meaningful jobs, an imbalanced criminal justice system, and a culture that ignores the consequences of single-parent homes. There will be moments when we will have to fight through racism to address these issues, but the longer our focus remains on racism, the longer it will take to get to substantive change.

There's also the fear to move the conversation beyond a White person's guilt and include the Black role in the problem and solution. Jerod Cherry, in a *Cleveland Plain Dealer* article from September 6, 2020, called "Healing America means changing our collective team culture," addresses this situation directly. Cherry is a former NFL player with three Super Bowl rings, so my sense is that he knows quite a bit about teamwork, personal sacrifice, and accountability. He talks about each of these areas from a Black societal perspective along with having the courage to put aside claims of victimhood to accelerate solution development.

Greed.

There is an adage in advertising circles that sex sells. The adage in our current environment is that police shootings sell. Racism now sells. White privilege now sells. It sells for the media, our politicians, community leaders, and special interest groups who align with whatever happens to be the crisis of the moment. Advisors within the

Obama administration championed the phrase "never let a good crisis go to waste." This crisis is no different. How much money is being raised on the back of this crisis and how much will go to real solutions is to be determined. Raising money may make a difference to the Black Lives Matter movement, but it remains to be seen if it will matter to Black lives. Shocking headlines are now the accepted practice for increasing ratings at the expense of accurate reporting.

Ignorance.

This crisis is heavy on misinformation and light on critical thinking. There is an expression called *argumentum ad ignorantiam*. It literally means "appeal to ignorance." Its premise is based on presenting an argument as fact, not based on its merits or reasoning, but presuming the opposing view will be ignorant and not be "at the ready" to argue otherwise. The opposing view loses the day even though their experience and instincts tell them there is a case to be made for an alternative conclusion. So, let us be at the ready with both sides of an issue. Let us not be ignorant of the need to hear more than one point of view. We need to develop a balanced conversation based on facts, circumstances, and reasoning. Hearing just one side of an argument is counterproductive whether it occurs at the dinner table, a local pub, or on cable TV.

The strategy of *argumentum ad ignorantiam* may make for an impressive monologue but it leads to horrific solutions.

The generation of my dad and mom was memorialized in a book by Tom Brokaw called *The Greatest Generation*. If we continue down the path we have currently set, my generation and those that follow will be labeled the Dumbest Generation(s). It is not because my parents' generation was any smarter, but once they recognized they were faced with a crisis that could deeply damage this country, they had the courage to admit to the issue and then muster the tenacity to fix it.

In the '40s it was about settling the great debate of continuing the U.S. policy of isolationism, the choice between avoiding war at all cost or fighting for freedom in Europe and Asia to protect our own. Japan helped with that decision, but once we were in, we were all in.

In the '60s, it was about a Democratic President, first Kennedy and then Johnson, and Republicans in Congress coming together to pass Civil Rights legislation.

In the '70s it was about abuse of power both in the White House and in the halls of our intelligence agencies.

Democrats and Republicans came together, saw this behavior for what it was—a threat to our democracy—and forced a president to resign and make changes to our intelligence agencies.

In the '80s, a threat to our standard of living enabled President Reagan, a Republican, together with a Democratic Speaker of the house, Tip O'Neil, to confront double-digit inflation, unemployment, and interest rates. Also, our military went from being a depleted fighting force to one that helped defeat the Soviet Union without firing a shot. Reagan got his tax cuts, regulatory changes, and military buildup; Tip got his spending programs. They had the confidence and courage to form a grand compromise, courage that our leaders sadly, both public and private, lack today.

If we are to replicate these efforts to find solutions, all sides will need to come together with clarity and determination to focus on this issue: to eliminate Black disadvantage. We need to put politics, particularly identity politics, on the back burner for a while until we get through this. Courage and confidence to deliver solutions the right way is sorely missed and needed.

The focus on eliminating White privilege will do nothing for Black America. Addition by subtraction never works. Our focus needs to be on eliminating *Black disadvantage.* Education, safe housing, meaningful employment, criminal justice reform, and changing the culture of single-parent homes would provide a giant leap forward.

Argumentum ad ignorantiam

The purpose of this writing is to address ignorance, to help promote a more balanced discussion that hopefully will help mitigate fear, shine a light on greed, and accelerate real change. Let us not allow false truths to be spread unchallenged due to ignorance by those on either side of the argument. It will only delay progress.

We need to have a candid, educated conversation. A conversation based on knowledge, with tolerance for thoughtful opposing viewpoints and without the fear of being labeled a racist or a socialist if we don't agree. We need to move from emotions based on surveys of one and misperceptions to understanding what is real and what is not. Until we do, nothing will get done.

Let us eliminate the fear and find the courage through knowledge to accept accomplishments of those on different sides of the conversation and admit to the shortcomings of those we support. We cannot continue to throw the good out with the bad; there just isn't enough good to start. Blind faith and complete trust in a leader or a cause will lead us all to blindly fall off the proverbial cliff.

Challenge this reading to give it staying power—and do not give in to surveys of one.

I ask that you *not accept* what follows as right or wrong. I ask that you think about what is written and then challenge it. If you claim to care, then invest some time and do your homework. Not only will you come away having better validated your truths held or discovered, you will also undoubtedly discover nuances not covered by this author that will add perspective to your conversations.

My only caveat is you look at both sides of an argument. Don't simply rest on what a friend told you or on surveys of one. One news outlet, one interview, one analyst. Listen to differing points of view. Watch CNN, MSNBC, and Fox News. Read the *New York Times*, the *Washington Post*, but also read the *Washington Times* and *Wall Street Journal* op-ed pages. Get on the Real Clear Politics website and get both sides from the same site. At the time of this writing it wasn't unusual to find a headline touting President Trump as an idiot and the next headline claiming he is a genius. Read both and then apply your critical thinking. And if your answer is you don't have time for this, then you'll be hard pressed to bring constructive dialogue to any conversation.

On the September 9, 2020, airing of *ABC News with David Muir*, one of Muir's intro headlines was about a teacher "dying from the virus; she had returned to the classroom two weeks ago." If you had stopped listening at that point or not delved deeper into this story, you would have thought she taught in a classroom full of children, contacted the virus, and tragically died within two weeks. But that wasn't the story at all. Turns out she was never in a classroom teaching during that time. The closest she got to students was teaching one virtual class. Her death was sad, but not caused by going back into the classroom with a room full of children. Drawing conclusions from headlines and surveys of one is dangerous and must stop. The Muir headline certainly got my attention, but the story behind the headline supported a different truth.

Beware of headline knowledge. In today's world, it is anything but.

> Socrates: *"The unexamined life is not worth living." "There is only one good, knowledge, and one evil, ignorance."*

Let's stop having the same unexamined conversation over and over. Money and mea culpas will not help. Structural changes will.

The conversation we are having today is 60 years old. We seem to have made some progress in the 1960s and '70s but not so much in the past 40 years. If all we do is dumb this conversation down to racism and money, our grandchildren will be having the same conversation and have a new word for "woke" to describe their come-to-Jesus moment.

I'm reminded of the movie *A Christmas Carol*, where the Ghost of Christmas Past introduces the greedy Ebenezer

Scrooge to two children, Ignorance and Want. Well, this is Christmas 2020, and if we're not careful, we will repeat the errors of the past and raise another generation of ignorance and want because we turned a blind eye to greed.

The good news: There are structural elements we can address to accelerate progress while we continue to tackle the blending of cultures.

Any business leader will tell you that when you merge two large organizations, blending corporate structures is very difficult, but the real challenge is blending corporate cultures.

To my White brothers and sisters, change is needed. To deny that will move us along to our country's demise by implosion.

To my Black brothers and sisters, to point the finger of blame primarily on White privilege is to invite another generation of disappointment, confusion, and failure.

Let's not be distracted by detours and naysayers. It is time for courage and confidence, for Black and White to begin meaningful, structural changes… *now*.

I recently read a piece from *Axios* that references a study that came out of the Samuel DuBois Cook Center on Social Equity, an organization whose existence is about racism and bias. The article details the ten myths of closing the wealth gap between White and Black America. Here is the overall theme of the ten myths:

*There are no actions that black Americans
can take unilaterally that will have much of an
effect on reducing the racial wealth gap. For
the gap to be closed, America must undergo a
vast social transformation produced by the
adoption of bold national policies, policies
that will forge a way forward by addressing,
finally, the long-standing consequences of
slavery, the Jim Crow years that followed, and
ongoing racism and discrimination that exist
in our society today.*

Yes, there is a wealth gap, but to me these ten myths say
that progress with Black America will be held back until we
address and instill a "vast social transformation." Will
someone please explain what exactly a "vast social
transformation" looks like and provide some type of timeline
or even steps to success? I doubt if a practical plan exists.

Every day we see Black Americans taking the initiative
and succeeding. Articles like this one from *Axios* don't help
them and it will not help the next generation who want to
succeed but are being told they cannot. The idea that a Black
man or woman is doomed until society changes is more than
a myth. It is a trap to hold back progress for Black America.
Sixty years from now we will be having the same
conversation if we buy into that myth.

Now, contrast this article with the one written by Jerod Cherry and you will find the difference between a roadmap toward progress and the *Axios* article, which is a roadmap to continuing the current state.

I have listed several pretenses in the next chapter that I believe inhibit meaningful conversation on progress made and progress that is achievable. I'm not trying to convince you of one side or the other, but I would like for you to see it through a lens not typically represented in today's media and to then come up with your own point of view based on knowledge and not information from a narrow sphere of reference.

Following my comments on these pretenses, I will report on three years of research, study, and conversations regarding one piece of this interwoven puzzle: single-parent homes. The adverse consequences on these homes have been catastrophic when weighing its effects on children, woman's health, the wealth gap, and the barriers they create for future generations. Fixing this will help enormously when addressing other pieces toward progress: education, safe neighborhoods, jobs, and criminal justice reform.

2. Let's Stop Pretending

To avoid having this same conversation in 60 years, let us stop pretending that:

- The United States is one of the most racist countries of our time.
- We are, for the first time, "woke".
- Most tragedies, including police shootings, are the result of a singular action.
- All White privilege is the same.
- In most cases it is about racism and not fixing significant structural issues.
- Throwing a lot of money at the problem will fix Black disadvantage.
- This is primarily a White person's problem and not a Black person's as well.
- Voting as a block for the past 60 years has helped the Black community.
- Police unions do its members a service by protecting problem cops.

- The Black community does itself justice by putting forth false narratives like "hands up, don't shoot".
- We have freedom of speech on this issue.
- People who deal in absolutes are helpful.
- The Black Lives Matter movement is sustainable.

Let's stop pretending: The United States is one of the most racist countries of our time

In an article published in the *Washington Post* in 2013, a headline reads "A fascinating map of the world's most and least racially tolerant countries." Two Swedish economists, in a World Values Study, set out to gauge whether economic freedom made people racist. It lists seven different tiers of racially tolerant countries, and the U.S. is in the lower strand among the most tolerant. The least tolerant country is India, with a smattering of other countries across the Middle East, Africa, and Asia among the various tiers of least tolerant.

Comparing us with Western Europe also shines light on where we are. A study published in *Sociological Science* looked at 200,000 applicants to identify discrimination at the hiring level. France had the highest discrimination rates, followed by Sweden. They found smaller differences among Great Britain, Canada, Belgium, the Netherlands, Norway, U.S., and Germany.

A couple of surveys an argument does not make, so let us look at some anecdotal evidence that suggest progress.

- In the past 60 years a Black president was elected for the first time (and he was reelected).
- In 1965, there were zero Black mayors. Today there are 39 in the top 100 cities.
- In 1965, only six members of the House of Representatives were Black; in 2019 fifty-two House members were Black.
- The first two African American Supreme Court justices were nominated and confirmed in the past 52 years.
- I doubt if you could find a major college or corporation today without a diversity department/initiative.
- The overwhelming majority of Americans, Black and White, are ready for change:
  - Every survey I have seen since May of 2020 shows anywhere from 60%–80% of Americans agree we need action in the U.S. to address change for Black America.
  - In a 2019 Pew Research Center survey, 84% of Black adults said that, in dealing with police, Blacks are generally treated less fairly than whites; 63% of Whites said the same.

Similarly, 87% of Blacks and 61% of Whites said the U.S. criminal justice system treats black people less fairly.

- Fifty years ago, if you saw an interracial couple walking down the street, you would get stares and whispers. Today, it rarely generates a second thought or glance.

- In the past three years the Trump administration has championed The First Step Act, created Opportunity Zones to help economically distressed neighborhoods, and signed a bill providing $250M per year to primarily Black colleges permanently each year.

- This, from Pew Research: "A record 3.8 million black immigrants live in the United States today, more than four times the number in 1980, according to a Pew Research Center analysis of U.S. Census Bureau data. Black immigrants now account for 8.7% of the nation's Black population, nearly triple their share in 1980. Rapid growth in the Black immigrant population is expected to continue. The Census Bureau projects that by 2060, 16.5% of U.S. blacks will be immigrants." If the U.S. is such a racist country, why would Black immigration continue to grow in the U.S.?

Dr. Phillip Atiba Goff, a social psychologist, wrote an article titled "To Fix Racism We Need to Start Measuring It." He argues that racism should be measured "as an accumulated pattern of behaviours that disadvantage one racial group and advantage another racial group, as well as the systems that facilitate that." Note: not based on surveys of one or simply random acts, but patterns. Let us target the areas that need improvement and not throw out the good along with the bad. I just gave you two data points that suggest the U.S. is not a racist country. No doubt racism exists in the U.S., both Black and White. But a racist country it is not. There is a difference. We have come a long way in 60 years to narrow the racial divide, but unfortunately not as well addressing the economic divide. That will take women and men with courage, tenacity, and knowledge.

Let's stop pretending: We are "woke" for the first time
The costliest generation of "woke" was of course the Civil War, when more than 300,000 Union soldiers lost their lives fighting for the right of the federal government to outlaw slavery. Laying down your life for a higher cause and another man goes well beyond woke; that is commitment and courage of the highest calling.
In the past 60 years we continued to have any number of woke moments:

- Equal Rights Act 1964 (War on Poverty)
- Civil Rights Act 1968 (prohibited housing discrimination)
- Equal Credit Opportunity Act 1974 (outlawed discrimination by creditors based on race)
- Community Reinvestment Act 1977 (outlawed redlining)
- Civil Rights Restoration Act of 1987 (all recipients of federal funds must comply with civil rights)
- Civil Rights Act of 1991 (provides the right of trial by jury for employment discrimination lawsuits)
- Violent Crime and Control and Law Enforcement Act 1995 (increased sentencing for hate crimes)
- Emmett Till Unresolved Civil Rights Crime Act (2007) (allows criminal cases of violent crimes committed against African Americans before 1970 to be reopened)
- Matthew Shepard and James Byrd Jr. Hate Crimes Prevention Act (2009) (allows federal authorities to investigate and prosecute hate crimes)
- There have been a host of presidential executive orders starting with the Emancipation Proclamation.
- Several federal commissions have been initiated including the Civil Rights Commission, Equal

Opportunity Commission, Head Start, and the Office of Fair Housing and Equal Opportunity.

My point is simply that racism in the U.S. has not been ignored. What has been ignored is the lack of progress of African Americans despite establishing laws, funding, electing Black men and woman to positions of power, and establishing government entities to direct dollars, policies, and laws. If we keep addressing this problem the same way (money, mea culpas, and bureaucrats), we will fail once again. We will not regulate our way out of this; we need to come together and have adults in the room to lead our way out of it, public and private. We need to recognize and then eliminate the fear, greed, and ignorance from our conversations. We need to uncover and implement meaningful structural changes and put in metrics to manage to success.

Let's stop pretending: Most tragedies, including police shootings, are the result of a singular act

There's a book called *Outliers* by Malcolm Gladwell. A very interesting read if you enjoy learning about things that may not always follow routine thought and rationality. One of those ideas surround how most tragedies come to pass. Consider an airline crash. Most would assume a mechanical malfunction, pilot error or perhaps weather, when they hear of a crash. But Mr. Gladwell points out that most significant tragedies are a combination of factors. A plane that starts out flying in bad weather combined with an inexperienced or poorly trained crew and finally a mechanical failure will lead to a tragedy. Addressing these shortcomings singularly, when there was time to mitigate the risks, would have avoided a potential plane crash. But if we don't, these three factors will come together to cause an unfortunate tragedy.

So too with police shootings. In Atlanta you had a classic example. What starts out as a DUI stop, for some reason takes far longer than it should, escalates when Rayshard Brooks grabbed a Taser from the officer and then attempts to shoot him. These actions then led to a poorly trained police officer—allowing Rayshard to steal his Taser, allowing the incident to escalate—to respond by shooting Rayshard. Clearly a lot went wrong with this police action. But this is clearly a death from many factors. Along with Mr. Brooks and the officer's actions, my guess is there was a breakdown in leadership and preparation as well, particularly when the country was on edge after George Floyd's murder.

Let's stop pretending that most police stops gone wrong are solely the fault of the police or a Black suspect. We have almost all felt the fear from a police officer, whether it is from police car lights in our rear-view mirror or something else. How we handle that fear is critical in minimizing its effects. How police handle fear and uncertainty when placed in a perceived dangerous situation needs to be addressed as well (and that danger is often very real: a police officer is 18.5 times more likely to be killed by a Black male than an unarmed Black male is killed by a police officer).

This, from a Malcolm Gladwell flashcard: "The reader can think of airplane crashes as outliers of failure in the same way that people like Bill Gates are successful outliers. They are rare, and when they do happen, it is because of a confluence of various seemingly unrelated factors."

When you look at the number of police interactions, a police shooting is very, very rare—and almost certainly a confluence of many factors. We need to look at the multiple factors and resist the over-simplistic view that the action or event is the police or suspect's fault. Instead, we need to address the red flags on both sides that will lead to long-term progress.

Let's stop pretending: All White privilege is the same
Included in this over-simplistic concept of White privilege are immigrants, first or even second generations of White heritage. They didn't prosper on the backs of Black America. Conversely, segments of America prospered on their backs. They didn't look down on Black America, for they were at the bottom of the economic ladder looking up as well. They were forced to live in ghettos called Little Italy or Chinatown

or South Boston (a home to many Irish immigrants). These neighborhoods had poverty, crime, and no one in years past would have accused the people in these neighborhoods as having possessed privilege.

Stop the identity politics. Segments of White America have and will continue to struggle and need to work hard to succeed. Some will succeed and some will fail. Perhaps a better metric is *economic* privilege?

Is there White privilege in this country? Yes. Do we all, those of us who are White, benefit from it in some degree? Yes. Do most of us flaunt that White privilege on a regular basis? No. Is it prevalent in all our lives? No. Where it does exist, let's target solutions instead of taking the intellectually lazy way out and brushing everyone with a broad stroke.

Is being White itself a form of racism? I think not. Racism is a human condition, not a White condition. Racism is acquired, in both Black and White communities; we are not born with it. To equate being White with being racist is racist unto itself. From Merriam-Webster: "a belief that race is the primary determinant of human traits and capacities and that racial differences produce an inherent superiority of a particular race."

To label a White person as being a racist simply based on one's race is literally the definition of racism.

Let's stop pretending: In most cases it is about racism and not fixing significant structural issues

About four years ago I came across statistics concerning the significant disadvantages that children face in homes with a single parent, regardless of race. More than 60% of African American households in Cleveland, and mirrored in most major cities around the country, are led by single parents, and most of those households are led by women. That led me down a path of research and conversation in hopes of learning more about Black disadvantage and why that cycle continues. Here are the foundational factors I found to lead us down the path of meaningful improvement:

1. Education. It is remarkable what an education will do on multiple levels, from lessening the odds of teen pregnancy to narrowing the chance of poverty, drug use, crime, and a host of other issues. If we don't fix education, the odds will continue to be stacked against Black youth. The biggest need is to develop child-centric solutions. You have politicians, bureaucrats, teacher unions, judges, and maybe a smattering of educators making decisions. They all have their agendas, and the real educators are outnumbered and outgunned when it comes to making real change. Perhaps the biggest example of this concerned the decisions made regarding

desegregation busing back in the 1970s. That was designed by politicians, supervised by judges, and implemented by bureaucrats. The objective was to improve inner city education and better integrate schools. It accomplished neither!

2. Safe housing. How many innocent children in Chicago, Cleveland, Atlanta, and New York City et al. must die at the hands of criminals before we really start walking the walk that Black Lives Matter? And beyond that, how much intimidation and fear do children live with each day, holding them back from getting a better education and a better life? You want a better future for Black America? How about starting with a safer today.

3. Jobs, quality jobs, and capital to support the entrepreneurial spirit. Over the past few pre-pandemic years, the rate of unemployment in Black communities came down. It would be interesting to pair that with a measurement on the quality of jobs. Investment in opportunity zones is another good sign. The pandemic is taking its toll on this progress and we need a focus to get back on track once we are through this. From the Cato Institute: "Economic growth does more to reduce poverty over time than

any government intervention. But it must be inclusive."

4. Changes to the criminal justice system should include everything from police bias and its contributory causes, to sentencing guidelines, to enforcing rules of prosecution, to how we handle inmates in maintaining a connection with their families. Many studies by the Vera Institute of Justice and others demonstrate how maintaining contact with family members while an inmate is in prison reduces the recidivism rate once they are released. A win for the inmate, the family, and our economy in not having to spend $31,000/year housing that returning inmate.

5. Fix the culture that marginalizes the incredible advantages of two-parent homes. The stats are clear. I will do a deeper dive in this area in the next chapters, but the incidence of poverty, teen pregnancy, infant mortality, school dropout rates, drug abuse et al. don't rise in percentages but in multiples in single-parent homes.

Even Barack Obama acknowledged and became an advocate for addressing this problem. This is from his Father's Day message in 2008:

> *"But if we are honest with ourselves, we'll admit that what too many fathers also are*

missing—missing from too many lives and too many homes. They have abandoned their responsibilities, acting like boys instead of men. And the foundation of our families are weaker because of it. You and I know how true this is in the African American community. We know that more than half of all Black children live in single-parent households, a number that has doubled—doubled—since we were children. We know the statistics—that children who grow up without a father are five times more likely to live in poverty and commit crime; nine times more likely to drop out of schools and 20 times more likely to end up in prison. They are more likely to have behavioral problems or run away from home or become teenage parents themselves. And the foundations of our community are weaker because of it."

And this line comes from his Father's Day proclamation in 2012:

"Every father bears a fundamental obligation to do right by their children."

We have the time, talent, and treasure as a nation to address all five areas. They are not independent of each other. A stable family life helps enormously with education and crime reduction. Safe housing will do the same. But we need people in the room with the experience, commitment, and courage to get these things done. Not politicians, bureaucrats, union leaders, or community activists, whose interests are aligned elsewhere.

Let's stop pretending: Throwing a lot of money at the problem will fix Black disadvantage

Since the start of the war on poverty in 1965, we have spent more than $20 trillion on welfare and any number of support programs. The rate of poverty has changed little within the Black community. As President Reagan once pointed out, "In the 1960s we declared war on poverty and poverty won." If Reagan knew this 33 years ago, how woke can we claim to be?

Reparations. ESPN ran a story back in 2015 that within two years of retirement, 78% of NFL players go broke. Within five years, 60% of NBA players go broke. The same can be said for lottery winners. What that tells me is that if people, regardless of color, are not prepared to handle money, even large sums of money, their fortunes, such as they may be, will wither away quickly. By simply giving out large packages of reparation money, direct or indirect, all you will do is create a cottage industry to separate that money from those receiving reparations, and that industry will act without conscious or remorse. Those NBA and NFL players were surrounded by advisors when they came into the league, and that didn't help many of these sudden millionaires hold onto their money. What makes you think the average, everyday man will be more prepared to handle that money? How about preparing people first to handle opportunity (education, safe housing, meaningful jobs, criminal justice reform, culture change)? If we don't do this, all you will do is put more money into the control of the bureaucrats and politicians, and only they will benefit.

Let's stop pretending: This is primarily a white person's problem and not a Black person's as well
When 60% of families in Cleveland or in just about any other big city are single-parent homes, that is a problem. We need to stop hiding from this fact. The next chapter again goes into this more deeply but pretending it isn't a huge issue makes no sense.

Black on Black crime is far deadlier and destructive than White on Black or Blue on Black. How are there not protests and rallies to bring awareness to this problem?

How do you ignore headlines like this one from ABC News, July 5, 2020?

The latest carnage in the Windy City came after a 20-month-old boy and a 10-year-old girl were among 14 people shot to death in Chicago last weekend, when 40 more were wounded.

Until you walk the walk that *all* Black Lives Matter, you will have cynics and deniers who will make this uphill battle much steeper, claiming that this is not a White problem but a Black problem, and they will be partly right.

Until the Black community takes a step back, has the courage and commitment to put the culture issue in play, all else will fail. How do I know? More than $20 trillion in welfare and other dollars spent over the past 60 years didn't work. A host of laws, commissions, executive orders didn't work. What will be done differently, how will outcomes improve, if the culture hasn't changed and giving education, safety, jobs, and justice reform isn't given a chance? And again, if your answer is money and mea culpas, been there, done that. Not a formula for progress.

Let's stop pretending: Voting as a block for the past 60 years has helped the Black community

In the past four years we have made some progress in mitigating Black disadvantage. The First Step Act, record low unemployment within the Black community, real wage growth for lower income Americans, permanent funding for Black Colleges stand out. In the next four years the time has come to hold President Biden and Congress accountable to do better. Results, not words. If not, it is time for the Black community to move on and look for alternatives. If you want change, then vote for change and not for just another talking head. Demand progress in education, safe housing, criminal justice reform, employment, and a culture that values families and children. Giving away 90% of your voting block every election cycle without measurable and meaningful progress is a recipe for a nothing burger, and that is exactly what you will continue to get.

Let's stop pretending: Police unions do its members a service by protecting problem cops

I get it that police unions need to stand with its members but not at the cost of putting most of its membership at risk, and we are at that point. That risk goes well beyond funding but now includes police safety and working conditions.

This is not something that will be done at a national level. Senator Tim Scott of South Carolina led a group in proposing a bill that had real change in it. It died, not because of disagreements of what was in the bill, but because the Democrats thought it didn't go far enough. And the House is equally guilty of putting politics over progress. I mentioned earlier that there have been tipping points over the past century bringing Democrats and Republicans together. I guess criminal justice reform has not made it to that level yet. All the bluster and outrage in Congress about justice reform for Black America is just that: bluster.

It will be up to the local governments and police departments to insist on change. Police unions and local leadership need to be part of the change. Simply taking away money and not changing the structure of how things get done will not help. It will only kick the can down the road, which is what we seem to be doing with everything, whether the issue is serious policy changes or budgets.

The continued policy of denial by police unions on the need for real change will continue to put the officers and profession at risk. What happened in Minneapolis with George Floyd will unfortunately happen again. But circumstances like this are rare. For police unions not to publicly condemn the police actions in this case and work hard transparently to avoid other like events is simply beyond the pale of reason and lacks the confidence and courage that city and union leadership must now engage.

Let's stop pretending: The Black community does itself justice by putting forth false narratives like "hands up, don't shoot"

The reaction and rioting after the Ferguson, Missouri, episode probably hurt the Black community's credibility more than anything a racist could have possibly done. We had protests and riots after activists, Black leaders, and the media all reported that an innocent Black man was shot after he raised his hands and started yelling don't shoot. Turns out that was a fabricated story, investigated and debunked by Eric Holder, a Black U.S. Attorney General who worked for a Black president, Barack Obama.

And it continues. The Pittsburgh Steelers put the name of a Black man shot by police on their helmets only to be made aware later that the man was involved in a drive-by shooting.

Police shot and killed a total of nine unarmed Black men in 2019. Police interactions with civilians are literally in the tens of millions. If you look at the headlines today, you will think Black men are being shot daily without cause. The media and Black leadership are undermining the credibility of this movement with exaggeration and sometimes false narratives.

The death of George Floyd was appropriately labeled an outrageous, tragic death. And there's no doubt that there's Black bias within police departments that needs to be addressed. But let us figure out why, and again going back to the *Outliers* story, it's most likely due to a confluence of reasons.

Let's stop pretending: We have freedom of speech on this issue

Freedom of speech is disappearing in this country. Growing up I would have not thought that possible. Today we seem to be afraid of an open and honest debate. I for one, and many people I've spoken with, try to completely avoid public conversation about the racism issue except with people we know well. Disagree with the basic principle of White privilege and systemic racism and you will be branded a racist and shut down.

You see editors of leading newspapers like the *New York Times* and *Philadelphia Inquirer* being asked to resign because they issue a phrase like "All Lives Matter," "Buildings Matter," or allowing an opposing point of view to be published in response to the rioting and destruction of property. Firing or forcing people to resign for a point of view you don't agree with is a big step toward a totalitarian media. The fact that every respectable member of the media is not up in arms about this is just mystifying. Freedom of speech and an independent media are pillars on which this country was built. These freedoms have led to many improvements in our society, from a woman's right to vote, to civil rights, to ending the Vietnam War. Take freedom of speech away and our society will bend to those who have the power of the bully pulpit.

I think Bari Weiss, a *New York Times* editor and columnist who felt forced to resign, expresses this best:

> *All this bodes ill, especially for independent-minded young writers and editors paying close attention to what they'll have to do to advance in their careers. Rule One: Speak your mind at your own peril. Rule Two: Never risk commissioning a story that goes against the narrative. Rule Three: Never believe an editor or publisher who urges you to go against the grain. Eventually, the publisher will cave to the mob, the editor will get fired or reassigned, and you'll be hung out to dry.*

Fear, ignorance, and greed:

Fear from those who know this is so wrong but are afraid to support columnist like Bari Weiss.

Ignorance for those subscribing to these publications without recognizing the breakdown of a free media will cost us all in the end, regardless of your political affiliation.

Greed from those who have turned media bias into an incredibly profitable business and have put their greed ahead of the American pillar of free speech that made their profession and this country great.

And make no mistake: They are destroying their profession.

As a result, we grow increasingly distrustful of the media. A Morning Consult poll in April, 2020, found that "The share of U.S. adults who said nine leading media outlets— including CBS and the *New York Times*—were credible has dropped roughly 9 percentage points since December 2016, from 60.6 percent to an average of 51.2 percent today. Last year, the average credibility rating sat at 55.4 percent." That is consistent with other media surveys like those from Pew Research and Gallup. In 1972, the first year Gallup measured trust in the media, 68% of Americans trusted the media. Only 41% today and of those only 13% have a great deal of trust and 28% a fair amount.

Almost as big a threat as the lack of tolerance for free speech in our media is the lack of free speech on our college campuses. Conservative speakers are being cancelled or deplatformed (shutting down a speaker or denying them access to a speaking venue) throughout this country on a regular basis. Simply do an Internet search on conservative speakers on college campuses and you will see the alarming number of speakers who have been cancelled or deplatformed.

How do we shape the next generation of critical thinking if people are limited to only one side of an issue? The answer is you don't. Students are being cheated by not being exposed to both sides of the issues and allowed to develop their critical thinking. They are being deprived of a far fuller education with the ability to develop independent thoughts without the fear of intimidation and condemnation. Allowing bullies to dictate policy is cowardice, whether on a playground or on our college campuses. And by the way, where are all those people whose "virtual signaling" was about anti-bullying a year or two ago?

Let's stop pretending: People who deal in absolutes are helpful

These are the people who are afraid of a conversation. They will label you a racist or socialist and shout you down if you disagree. They fear listening and are terrified that there may be validity to an opposing point of view. When you ask a question, they will give you a long eloquent monologue that often has nothing to do with your question. They will quote "facts" with the assumption of an *argumentum ad ignorantiam*. They will insist a particular person or cause is always right or always wrong.

These people are not helpful and are only feeding their egos and/or their greed. Many can be found across the cable news spectrum. If you can predict the answer of a pundit no matter the issue, why waste your time? They are less likely to add to a meaningful conservation and far more likely to instill fear, greed, and ignorance.

Balance in life is a beautiful thing, whether it is your diet, your work/life arrangement, or your politics.

Let's stop pretending: The Black Lives Matter movement is sustainable

The focus of Black Lives Matters is so narrow that it has little chance of being a sustained movement. By narrow I mean the only Black lives that seem to matter are the ones who make the headlines and generate donations. The thousands of Black lives, many of them children, who die on the streets because of Black on Black crime don't seem to matter. The Black police officer who was killed because of the rioting didn't seem to matter. The safety, security, and living conditions of Black lives don't seem to matter.

I saw a mention on the BLM website that they were joined by 60 celebrities for one of their efforts. That support will be fleeting. The support from those 60 celebrities and their colleagues will vanish as they move on to the next trendy cause in their effort to continue "virtue signaling." Remember their support about #metoo? Gone. This year, Bill Clinton had a starring role at the Democratic National

Convention. Anti-bullying was also a favorite of the celeb class but bullying now appears to be okay if directed at certain segments of our society. Next year, who knows, but most likely it will not be about Black lives.

BLM's challenge to the nuclear family is a *destructive distraction*. We have always needed a community to help families thrive. Those communities were there to support core values along with the building blocks of education, family, safety, and economic opportunity. Communities were there to support mothers and fathers, not supplant them.

For generations people have fought wars to avoid being told how to live their lives and raise their children. Communism and socialism consistently fail in large part for this reason. Germany tried this in the 1930s with tragic outcomes. Are there any examples of where this has been tried and worked? Before we enter another generation of trial and failure, where are the plans and what forms of evidence are there to support this experiment?

The fact is we have already started down that road, providing meals, childcare, clothing, housing to underprivileged children and their families. And once again I will quote President Reagan. "We declared war on poverty and poverty won." Let's not lose again.

To eliminate the wealth gap and black disadvantage, you will need to become an equal, not an island.

Until there is a broader acceptance that all Black lives matter within a society where all lives matter, any Black movement will be an island that will go the way of the Black Panthers. They will have their day in the sun, but that day will set with nothing to sustain them for the next.

One other note. Corporate America does Black lives no favor in creating islands. Goodyear initially banning Blue Lives Matter support but allowing support for Black Lives Matter is just another way to separate and delay equality.

3. What's Next

In the previous chapters we noted five areas that consistently rise as keys to help mitigate Black disadvantage and the wealth gap in America: education, safe housing, jobs, criminal justice reform, and a culture shift that promotes two-parent homes. On the remaining pages of this book, allow me to focus on the last of these issues: two-parent homes.

I focus on this issue for three reasons:

1. Reversing this trend of rising single-parent homes will make improvements exponentially easier in education, safer neighborhoods, jobs, and incarceration rates. Conversely, a lack of progress will make an uphill battle much steeper.

2. The events in the spring and summer of 2020 have heightened awareness of the need to narrow the health and wealth gaps in this country. A clear correlation exists that reducing single-parent homes will reduce the wealth and health gaps.

3. This is a topic that I have studied for the past three years and feel it now timely in sharing what I have learned.

What follows is A Case for Fatherhood: why it is so important for fathers to be present in the home, and A Case for Change: building awareness for a practical approach to help move this effort forward.

Each will start with a summary followed by a more detailed presentation. The summary will provide points of reference. The detail will provide greater depth to your conversations. After three years of study, I'm convinced that without meaningful and measurable interventions surrounding single-parent homes, achieving significant progress toward eliminating, or even reducing, Black disadvantage will be tenuous.

4. A Case for Fatherhood

The advantages of a two-parent home are significant for children, mothers, and their communities. The negative outcomes of single-parent homes align very closely with what is generally seen as Black disadvantages: increased poverty, poor health, a widening wealth gap. and greater dependence on public assistance.

Here is a quick summary of why it is so important to have active, engaged fathers.

There are significant personal costs for children living in single-parent homes. The risk of poverty, teen pregnancies, infant mortality, obesity, dropping out of school, going to prison, drug and alcohol abuse rise not in percentages but in multiples with children in single-parent homes.

There are significant economic costs in public support of single-parent homes:

- More than $100 billion dollars per year in federal spending to support single-parent homes

- Estimates range from $100 billion to $500 billion in direct and indirect costs per year from federal, state, and local governments

There is a significant wealth gap between female-headed, single-family homes and two-parent homes, particularly for those who never marry.

- *In 2011, children living in female-headed homes with no spouse present had a poverty rate of 47.6%. This is over four times the rate for children living in married couple families.* [Source: U.S. Department of Health & Human Services (2012). Information on poverty and income statistics: A summary of 2012 current population survey data]

- The poverty rate is double for never-married mothers compared with separated or divorced mothers

There are significant health issues associated with women heading up single-parent homes.

- Studies in the U.S. and Canada indicate that single moms face greater risks of anxiety, depression, and drug abuse.

Single moms, who head most single-parent homes, agree that we have a significant problem.

- Moms agree: In a national survey *"93% of the respondents to the mothers survey agreed (67%*

strongly) that there is a father-absence crisis in the United States today"

- Fathers not living with mothers receive overwhelmingly low marks compared to fathers living in the home, whether married or cohabiting

- *Asked to rate the importance of six possible places that might help fathers be better dads, the respondents as a whole placed the most importance on "churches and other communities of faith," followed closely by schools, then by "community-based organizations." The highest rating ("very important") was given frequently to "churches…" even by those respondents who said that they were "not at all religious" (58 percent) and "not very religious" (72 percent)—*national survey of American mothers in 2008 conducted by Norval Glenn and Barbara Dafoe Whitehead

The Slightly Longer Version

"It is easier to build strong children than to repair broken men" – Frederick Douglass, an American social reformer, abolitionist, orator, writer, statesman, and, for a time, slave

The following figures, and most of the numbers I will reference, have as their source U.S. Census Bureau statistics. I came across identical or very similar figures from a variety of sources.

Single Parent Homes – What is it costing us?

Today, almost one in four children live without a father in the home. It has not always been this way. In 1968, 8% of children lived in a single-parent home, which is an increase of 300% in just over 50 years.

Here are the costs as a result of this dramatic increase.

Personal Costs

- Children living in fatherless homes are at a tremendous disadvantage and are much more likely to incur significant challenges literally from before the time they are born. These disadvantages occur not in percentage increases, but in multiples. From the National Fatherhood Initiative:
  - Four times greater risk of poverty
  - Two times greater risk of infant mortality
  - Seven times more likely to become pregnant as a teen
  - Two times more likely to suffer obesity
  - Two times more likely to drop out of high school

- More likely to go to prison, abuse drugs and alcohol, and face abuse/neglect

Economic Costs

- The most comprehensive study on the economics of fatherless homes that I found was done by two professors at the University of Virginia, Steven L. Nock and Christopher J. Einolf. Their research showed that $99.8 billion was spent by the federal government in 2006 in providing assistance to father absent families. They based this on the amount the federal government spent on "thirteen means-tested benefit programs and on child support enforcement for single mothers. These programs include the Earned Income Tax Credit, Temporary Assistance for Needy Families (TANF), child support enforcement, good and nutrition programs, housing programs, Medicaid, and the State Children's Health Insurance Plan (SCHIP)."

- This study also concluded that "between 1960 and 2006, the number of children living in single-mother families went from 8 percent to 23.3 percent," and 34 percent of children currently live absent their biological father."

These numbers are taken from a study through the National Fatherhood initiative called the One Hundred Billion Dollar Man. These are not isolated figures.

In a study titled "The Taxpayer Costs of Divorcee and Unwed Childbearing," it concluded that "based on the methodology, we estimate that family fragmentation costs U.S. taxpayers at least $112 billion each and every year, or more than $1 trillion each decade."

I have seen other studies that estimate the costs of both direct and indirect costs can reach as high as $500 billion per year.

"For the man with the hammer, everything looks like a nail" – **Mark Twain**

The government answer to many of these issues is a new program, a bigger budget, but not a focus on primary causation of the problem of single-parent homes. There are a lot of people out there doing great work trying to overcome the issues brought on by fatherless homes. I have spoken to a number of people at the local, state, and national level, whether in a role with a government entity or a nonprofit. All are working hard to make incremental improvements. But those who I've spoken to will tell you that while they are making progress, there's so much more we could be doing to accelerate progress if we raised the awareness of the issue and gained the attention of those who are able to make a difference via policy, programs, and media.

In the end we must ask ourselves what is the $100B plus we spend each year doing for those in need.

Income Inequality

There's lots of chatter about the wealth gap:

"In 2011, children living in female-headed homes with no spouse present had a poverty rate of 47.6%. This is over four times the rate for children living in married couple families." [Source: U.S. Department of Health & Human Services (2012). Information on poverty and income statistics: A summary of 2012 current population survey data.]

Along with the personal and economic costs of fatherless homes, another side effect of the father absent home is economic inequality. How this has grown is reflected in many publications. Here are a few examples.

This is from the *NewBostonPost*:

Data from the Census Bureau, analyzed by the U.S. Department of Health and Human Services, shows that gulf in income between married-couple households and fatherless families is enormous. In fact, in 2013, the poverty rate among children in female-headed families with no spouse present was

45.8 percent—more than four times that of children
in married-couple families (9.5 percent).
But it is not just conservatives who recognize that
fatherlessness and poverty go hand in hand.
Even Barack Obama has made a point of noting on
more than one occasion that "children who grow
up without a father ... are five times more likely to
live in poverty and nine times more likely to drop
out of school" than children with fathers in the
home.

The following graph also points out the big difference in poverty rates between those moms who never married and those who are divorced or separated.

MASSACHUSETTS CHILDREN IN POVERTY

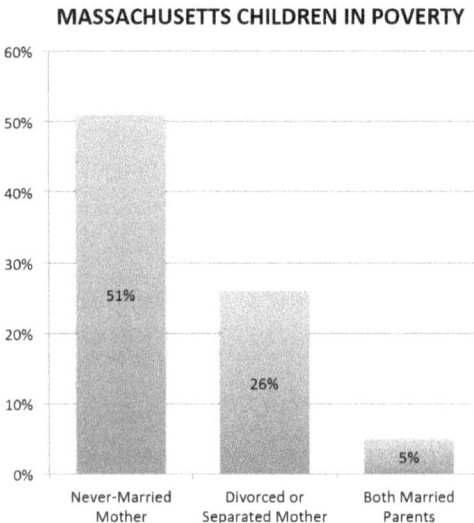

Chart courtesy of MFI; data source: National Survey of Children's Health (NSCH)

Despite the heroic efforts by many single mothers (and the success of many), the statistics clearly demonstrate the economic void that results when a father is not present in the home.

According to data analyzed by the Massachusetts Family Institute, in 2013, married-couple families in Massachusetts had a median annual income of more than $114,376—almost 75 percent higher than the $26,999 median annual income for Massachusetts female-headed households with children. The rate of child poverty in Massachusetts homes where the mother has never been married is even worse—51 percent of these children live at or below the poverty line.

Father-absent homes have little margin for error when economic challenges arise.

Women's Health

There are several studies that link single moms to increased risks of depression, anxiety, and drug abuse. A lack of access to health care and poverty are contributing factors to these problems, which are also more prevalent among single moms.

Beyond the research, common sense plays here as well, especially for anyone who has been a parent. Lacking a second parent in the home means a lot more work for the single parent, more stress in decision making, and more anxiety in not being able to do the things you know need to be done, due to a lack of time, money, and/or energy.

The Fragile Family and Child Well Being study notes that mothers in single-parent homes are more likely to suffer from depression and more likely to report drug abuse. A conclusion can easily be made that a mother's health needs to be added to the list of adverse consequences of fatherless homes.

A study out of Canada found nearly the same results as the Fragile Family and Child Well Being study:

Given the significant social and economic disadvantage faced by many single-parent mothers, researchers have become interested in the health consequences of this increasingly more common family structure. Data from Canada, Great Britain, and the United States have consistently shown that single mothers are at increased risk for psychological distress and psychiatric disorder(s). For example, Cairney et al., using a large nationally representative sample of Canadians, found that single mothers were about twice as likely to have suffered an episode of major depression in the previous year than married mothers. In another more recent study, again using a sample from Canada, Lipman et al. also found higher rates of 12-month and lifetime affective/anxiety and substance-use disorders in single mothers as compared to married mothers.

Single Moms Agree: We have a problem

There is always a story behind the numbers, and I think this would be a good time to hear the voice of the single moms. This is the most comprehensive viewpoint of single moms that I've found. The headline from a national survey of American mothers in 2008, conducted by Norval Glenn and Barbara Dafoe Whitehead, is that "93% of the respondents to the mothers survey agreed (67% strongly) that there is a father-absence crisis in the United States today." Here are some other items of note.

- *The mothers' appraisals of the performance of fathers differed greatly according to whether or not the mother was married to or lived with the father. The mothers who lived with the fathers, including those cohabiting but not married, gave overwhelmingly high marks to the fathers, while those mothers not living with the fathers reported, on average, extremely negative views.*

- *The mothers not living with the fathers reported very low satisfaction with the fathers who had taken on new romantic, marital, or stepfather relationships. With each additional relationship or responsibility, the survey shows, these mothers were progressively less satisfied with the fathers' parenting.*
  - Something else to consider. I had a conversation with an inner-city Black minister and asked the question if he thought that fathers start out choosing not to support their children or if it was due to their specific circumstances. He felt that very few start out not wanting to do the right thing and support their children. He then went through the list of interruptions in their lives like a loss of a job or incarceration that prevented them from doing all that they wanted to do. New relationships are also a factor.
- *The survey yielded evidence that strong religious beliefs, values, and commitments are conducive to good fathering whether or not the father lives with the mother.*

- During the summer of 2018, Rahm Emmanuel, former Mayor of Chicago, responded to a question about the causes of the violence in his city resulting in over 500 murders on the streets of Chicago each year. He mentioned, among other things, that a breakdown in faith and family are a big part of this problem. He was vilified for this statement. The time has come to stop hiding and admit that a breakdown in faith and family is not a good thing for this country whether in the home or on our city streets and is contributing to the problem.

- *The mothers reported less satisfaction with the fathers of teenage children than with the fathers of younger children. Only 28 percent of the mothers of teenage offspring reported that the father-child relationship was "very close and warm," compared with 38 percent for children ages 6–12, and 57 percent for those ages 0–5.*
  - It is not a coincidence that the satisfaction level for fathers with teenage children is only half of that for fathers with children ages 0–5. Most research shows that by age 5, half of non-resident

fathers begin to disappear. Check out a study titled "The Fragile Families and Child Wellbeing Study" if you want to take a deeper dive into these numbers and how non-married fathers, resident and non-resident fathers go away in time.

- *A majority of the mothers agreed that another man could be an adequate substitute for an absent or uninvolved father with twice as large a percentage of the mothers not living with the fathers agreeing that fathers are replicable. It is not clear however, whether these respondents thought that adequate substitution for fathers is likely or common.*
  - o The idea that a father is replaceable is not the question but how likely is it to happen. I had a conversation with a gentleman from the United Kingdom regarding this issue. He went as far as to say that moms and dads, although not preferable, are replaceable. He cited adoption policies and its many successes. But after a very brief pause, he followed up that even though it is possible, the probability of replacing mothers or fathers in large numbers is so small that the

argument is not a serious one. Replacing a father is a possibility, but not a probability.

- *Ninety-three percent of the respondents to the mothers survey agreed (67 percent strongly) that there is a father absence crisis in the United States today. This is very similar to the 91 percent of the respondents to the fathers survey who agreed (62 percent strongly) that there is such a crisis.* [The reference to the fathers' survey here is the 2006 survey released by the National Fatherhood Initiative, A National Survey of Dad's Attitudes on Fathering]
  - o This goes back to my first question: If there is such a recognition by the people who this problem touches, that there is a father absence problem, why the void of conversation and action? It baffled me when I asked that question for the first time at the start of this journey, and it still does today.
- *Asked to rate the importance of six possible places that might help fathers be better dads, the respondents as a whole placed the most importance on "churches and other*

communities of faith," followed closely by schools, then by "community-based organizations." The highest rating ("very important") was given frequently to "churches…" even by those respondents who said that they were "not at all religious" (58 percent) and "not very religious" (72 percent).

o The folks who lambasted Rahm Emmanuel should have looked at this survey. I'm not sure that faith alone is the reason churches finish number one, but I believe, along with family, it is a place where many of us get our moral compass. Someone once told me, and I have seen this play out repeatedly in my 68 years, that we are products of our reading and our experiences. If the family is breaking down and we are less likely to be affiliated with a faith, where will our children get that moral compass? Has it come down to relying on the Internet, social media, or what children learn on the school bus on the way home? How scary is that?

5. A Case for Change

The previous chapter focused on the case for fatherhood by chronicling the significant disadvantages single moms and children of single moms face, thereby continuing the cycle of Black disadvantage.

This chapter focuses on the case for change. There is no magic bullet. But there are four tangible and specific areas that have accelerated the surge in single-parent homes. The case for reversing these policies and impacting social change is a case to reverse the significant disadvantages of single-parent homes.

Summary:
There are four accelerants that have contributed to the explosion of single-parent homes:

1. The War on Poverty launched in 1965. The correlation is clear that single-parent homes started their upward trajectory during that time. You will find lots of evidence from a variety of sources, but this headline gives you a snapshot how the War on

Poverty has been linked to the start of the modern day issue of single family homes: "7 Ways the War on Poverty Destroyed Black Fatherhood" (from *Atlanta Black Star*).

2. Crime and incarceration policies have separated many more children in the past 60 years from their parents, and it is not just men:

   a. "Between 1991 and midyear 2007, parents held in state and federal prisons increased by 79% (357,300 parents). Children of incarcerated parents increased by 80% (761,000 children) during this period. The most rapid growth in the number of parents held in the nation's prisons and their children occurred between 1991 and 1997 (both up 44%). From 1997 to midyear 2007, the number of parents and children continued to grow, but at a slower pace (both up 25%)." – U.S. Department of Justice, Bureau of Justice Statistics, August 2008 and revised in 2010.

   b. "The number of women in prison increased by 587% between 1980 and 2011, rising from 15,118 to 111,387" – Rutgers University study, Resource Center on Children & Families of the Incarcerated in 2014.

c. Once in prison, a lack of importance placed on the inmate maintaining family contact fails to take advantage of an opportunity to reduce recidivism rates.

3. Child custodial and support policies often hinder family development and drive a wedge between the father and single mother:

   a. In many states a father has no custodial rights when his child is born out of wedlock. He must go to court for visitation and custodial rights.

   b. Child-support polices often drive fathers away when unable to pay child support. They are threatened with jail or the loss of their driver's license. Threats may work for a "deadbeat" dad but will only serve to provide another barrier for a "dead broke" dad to engage with his children.

4. Cultural Shift

   a. A number of societal changes have contributed to the problem.

      i. Cultural misperceptions brought on by the War on Poverty and other polices

      ii. A lack of awareness and education on what are the consequences of single-parent homes affecting wealth, health, and opportunities to succeed

iii. Lack of candor from our public, private, and cultural leadership, acknowledging the consequences of single-parent homes

iv. The media's attempt to mask the true outcomes of single-parent homes

v. Devaluing our children—my take on six specific areas that I believe demonstrates a lack of valuing our children and their futures

This is a 60-year problem—and it isn't just about the Black community.

Since the 1960s the number of single-parent households have grown significantly. Fatherless homes are caused primarily by one of four primary reasons:

- Fathers leaving the home after marriage
- Death of a spouse
- Divorce
- Simply choosing not to get married

The first two have been relatively stable since the 1960s. Divorce rates have flattened out over the past two decades. The last one, simply choosing not to get married, has exploded and is the primary reason fatherless homes have grown from 4 million in 1968 to 16.8 million in 2017.

In the 1960s, men didn't suddenly decide to stop getting married and support their families. Nor did women just decide fathers were not a necessity. Certain structural changes occurred to incentivize and accelerate this phenomenon. And just as these were created with unintended consequences, they can be reversed. In having the casual conversations about our single-parent crisis, I've heard people say a number of times "So what are we supposed to do, make people get married?" No, but along with building awareness of just how big this impacts our children and single parents, there are four structural areas that need to be challenged to begin to reverse the impact of single-parent homes.

1. The War on Poverty starting in 1964 and the false assumptions that went with these programs.
2. Incarceration rates, starting with mass incarceration policies in the 1980s, accelerated in the 1990s with the passage of the Violent Crime Control and Law Enforcement Act, a bipartisan effort.
3. Custodial, child support policies.
4. Cultural changes.

Let us look at each of these and opportunities for change.

War on Poverty

The War on Poverty has had enormous unintended consequences. People have known for decades that this so-called War on Poverty was always a weak and ineffective attempt at fixing the problems, including welfare reform in 1996.

Unlike the previous chapter, where numbers are easily calculated and accessed, the War on Poverty and its negative effects are a bit blurry in directly relating numbers to numbers, but it's very easy to find an abundance of evidence linking its negative impact. Here are a variety of publications from different media and political viewpoints that are all telling the same story. There are differences in how real poverty rates are calculated within a couple of these studies, but the conclusions are all the same.

From *The American Conservative* [article published in 2016]:

"Marriage rejection rooted in the 1960s has real ramifications: among adults who are 34 years old or younger, some 46 percent have never been married.

This syndrome had perhaps its most profound impact in some of America's most difficult neighborhoods, where unparalleled family breakdown is, in part, the sad result of Lyndon Johnson's well-meaning miscalculations. We are living through the collapse of the traditional family and marriage as the norm and expectation for millions of Americans, especially in low-income communities.

Writer Myron Magnet observed that the "dream" of the Great Society has become a "nightmare" for the very people that the Great Society was designed to help. Poverty and single-mother childbearing were both higher after the Great Society than before, and the number of intact families has declined significantly."

This is not a race issue. Rates of children born out of wedlock have been on a similar trajectory whether White or Black since the 1960s and for Hispanic children since tracking started in the late '80s. Looking at this merely through a racial lens will be an attempt to divert the conversation away from its core issue: fatherless homes and its adverse consequences on our children, Black, White, or Brown.

The following graph, again based on U.S. Census data, illustrates this point.

CHART 10

Growth of Unwed Childbearing by Race in the United States, 1931-2008

PERCENTAGE OF CHILDREN
BORN OUT OF WEDLOCK

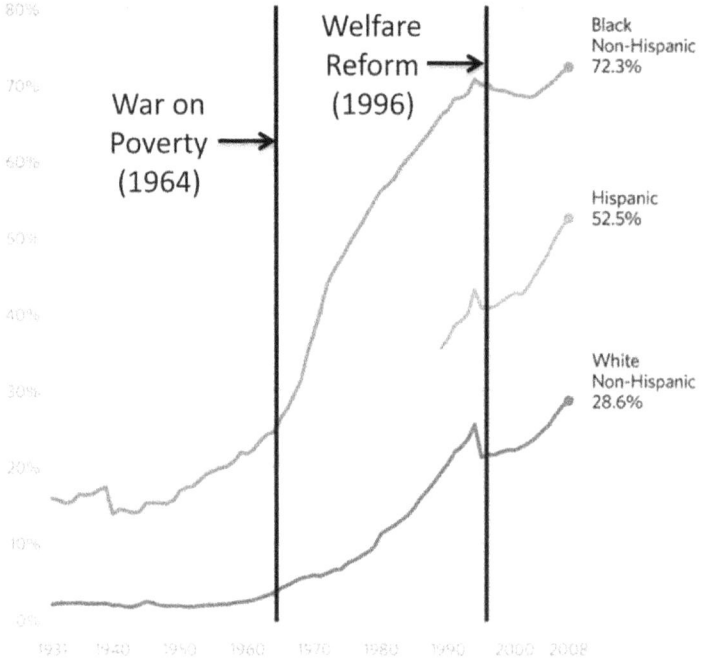

War on
Poverty →
(1964)

Welfare
Reform →
(1996)

Black
Non-Hispanic
72.3%

Hispanic
52.5%

White
Non-Hispanic
28.6%

80%

70%

60%

50%

40%

30%

20%

10%

0%

1931   1940   1950   1960   1970   1980   1990   2000 2008

Source: U.S. Government, U.S. Census Bureau, and National Center for Health Statistics.

SR 117 ☎ heritage.org

Something else to consider in negating this as a race issue. "Children from low-income, two-parent families outperform students from high-income, single-parent homes. Almost twice as many high achievers come from two-parent homes as one-parent homes." One-Parent

Families and Their Children, Charles F. Kettering
Foundation, 1990.

This information below is from the Cato Institute, written
by Michael Tanner. I'm not familiar with Tanner's work, but
he seems to capture what I have surmised from a variety of
sources and puts it into words much better than I.

*President Johnson himself called for something more
than simply fighting material poverty. The War on
Poverty was created not only to meet the 'basic needs" of
those in poverty, but also to "replace despair with
opportunity." Yet in focusing on the material aspects of
poverty, we have neglected the more important aspects of
human flourishing. Our tax and spending policies should
be better designed to enable every person to attain their
full potential, to be capable of being all that they can be.*

Tanner goes on to make recommendations in the areas of
reforming the criminal justice system (which we will get to
next) and its war on drugs, along with suggestions on
education, housing, and banking reforms. I'm not sure if his
suggestions and recommendations are the right ones, but the
conversation he advocates is spot on. His conclusion below
talks about an issue that got Bill Clinton elected, "It's the
Economy, Stupid." But what President Clinton forgot is that
the economy needed to be inclusive. Legislation and policies

like the 1994 crime bill did far more to harm the inclusion principle than it helped. More from Tanner:

> *Economic growth does more to reduce poverty over time than any government intervention. But that growth must be inclusive. We should also make it easier for the poor to find work today by eliminating regulations, licensure, zoning, and other laws that make it harder for the poor to find jobs or start a business.*

Regardless of your politics, President Trump seems to have addressed a number of these areas (criminal justice reform, job creation, eliminating regulations). We need to give credit where credit is due and build on success and not continually unwind the good from administration to administration.

Our support policies should build on family growth and progress, not penalize it. A recent report by the American Enterprise Institute shows that families with incomes of between $40,000 and $50,000 are most impacted by the marriage penalty. We need to change this penalty to an incentive. The $40,000–$50,000 income point should be something for families to build on to help couples get to the next income level, freeing themselves of government reliance and influence as well as achieving a higher standard of living.

Eliminating the marriage penalty within our support and welfare programs is desperately needed. We addressed the marriage penalty issue for tax purposes through the Tax Cuts and Jobs Act and other actions. It is now time to address the marriage penalty for assistance programs as well. Instead of penalizing marriage, we need to reward household growth.

Search the Internet for "war on poverty and fatherless families" and you will see scores of articles across a number of publication genres and categories—Black, White, conservative, libertarian, liberal—that catalog the failings of the War on Poverty. It is time for a serious conversation about our policies and where we go from here.

An effort to simply provide single moms a bare subsistence level to get by and hope that it will lead to progress is a recipe for continued failure. Hope is not a strategy, but policies that promote and reward progress are. We need to look at every opportunity to incentivize family, education, employment, and individual accomplishment.

I close on this topic with two thoughts. First, a thought of what a program's intent should be from a *National Review* Symposium. Second, a warning from President Franklin D. Roosevelt from more than 80 years ago.

This, from John Archambault, speaking at the *National Review* Symposium titled "The War on Poverty at age 50":

*Our country is better when we have a meaningful
safety net. The most prosperous nation in the history
of the world should provide basic protections for the
most vulnerable. But that safety net was intended to
be effective, affordable, focused, and committed to
moving people toward self-sufficiency. As we mark
the 50th anniversary of President Johnson's War on
Poverty, we see how far off the mark we are from his
attempt to move beyond the "Kennedy legacy."*

Franklin D. Roosevelt, the State of the Union Address,
January 4, 1935. This, from the man who was the architect of
the New Deal, a precursor to Johnson's Great New Society
and the War on Poverty.

*The lessons of history, confirmed by the evidence
immediately before me, show conclusively that
continued dependence upon relief induces a spiritual
and moral disintegration fundamentally destructive
to the national fiber. To dole out relief in this way is
to administer a narcotic, a subtle destroyer of the
human spirit. It is inimical to the dictates of sound
policy. It is in violation of the traditions of America.*

Our War on Poverty should be a safety net and one that
helps build a foundation for a better life, not a way of life.

Incarceration Policies

The previous chart illustrates the dramatic acceleration of unwed childbearing beginning in the 1960s with the start of the War on Poverty. This wave was also influenced by the start of mass incarceration policies in the 1980s. As an example, a Rutgers University study, Resource Center on Children & Families of the Incarcerated in 2014, notes, "The number of women in prison increased by 587% between 1980 and 2011, rising from 15,118 to 111,387." The impact of our incarceration policies intensified in the 1990s with the passage of the Violent Crime Control and Law Enforcement Act of 1994. I don't think it was the DNA of women, or men that changed, making them more prone to commit crimes, but somehow it was determined that incarcerating six times the number of women over a 30-year period was a good thing.

The Violent Crime Control and Law Enforcement Act of 1994 was the largest crime control package in the history of the U.S. at $30 billion. This summary is from the U.S. Department of justice:

The Violent Crime Control and Law Enforcement Act of 1994 represents the bipartisan product of six years of hard work. It is the largest crime bill in the history of the country and will provide for 100,000 new police officers, $9.7 billion in funding for prisons and $6.1 billion in funding for prevention

programs, which were designed with significant
input from experienced police officers. The Act also
significantly expands the government's ability to
deal with problems caused by criminal aliens. The
Crime Bill provides $2.6 billion in additional
funding for the FBI, DEA, INS, United States
Attorneys, and other Justice Department
components, as well as the Federal courts and the
Treasury Department.

Much like welfare reform in 1996, it addressed the
numbers but did little to improve the plight of those that got
caught up in the system. The Violent Crime Control and Law
Enforcement Act of 1994 addressed mandatory sentences,
establishing some uniformity and a three-strike rule. But it
did little to help alleviate the already growing incarceration
problem, its causes, crime and misjudgment, even though
$6.1 billion was designated for prevention programs. You
read this release above from the Department of Justice and
you get the impression this was a much needed and positive
piece of legislation. There were positives that came out of
this legislation to help reduce crime, but at what cost to a
piece of our social structure that had already taken several
policy hits. And once we saw the negative side of it, what did
we do to reverse these unwanted consequences?

So, what resulted from this aggressive stance on mass incarceration? This, from the U.S. Department of Justice, Bureau of Justice Statistics, August 2008, and revised in 2010:

Between 1991 and midyear 2007, parents held in state and federal prisons increased by 79% (357,300 parents). Children of incarcerated parents increased by 80% (761,000 children), during this period. The most rapid growth in the number of parents held in the nation's prisons and their children occurred between 1991 and 1997 (both up 44%). From 1997 to midyear 2007, the number of parents and children continued to grow, but at a slower pace (both up 25%).

Parents held in state prisons increased from 413,100 in 1991 to 686,000 at midyear 2007. Children of parents in state prison increased from 860,300 to 1,427,500 during this period. The largest growth in the number of parents (up 40%) held in state prison and their children (up 42%) occurred between 1991 and 1997, compared to a 19% increase for parents and a 17% increase for their children between 1997 and midyear 2007.

The number of children under age 18 with a mother in prison more than doubled since 1991 the nation's prisons held approximately 744,200 fathers and 65,600 mothers at midyear 2007. Fathers in prison reported having 1,559,200 children; mothers reported 147,400. Since 1991, the number of children with a mother in prison has more than doubled, up 131%. The number of children with a father in prison has grown by 77%. This finding reflects a faster rate of growth in the number of mothers held in state and federal prisons (up 122%), compared to the number of fathers (up 76%) between 1991 and midyear 2007.

Its impact on youth education is dramatic; from *Prison Legal News*, February 2017:

According to the Pew report, only 15 percent of children with an incarcerated father, and 2 percent with an incarcerated mother, graduate from college. For comparison, the college graduation rate for children without an incarcerated parent is 40 percent.

The Pew study noted that new and effective programs are needed to mitigate the harm associated with parental incarceration. The researchers specifically recommended that policymakers make it easier for children to maintain positive relationships with their parents during incarceration, and encouraged more child-friendly visiting areas to mitigate some of the anxiety and fear that many children experience when visiting a parent in prison.

The Rutgers article illustrates just how hard it is to maintain a relationship between incarcerated parents and children: "62% of parents in state prisons and 84% of parents in federal prisons are held over 100 miles away from their residence. 43% of parents in federal prisons are held over 500 miles away from their last residence."

There is promise of a better tomorrow if we do this right. Here's an example from the U.S. Department of Health and Human Services.

Most men plan to live with their families upon release, and those who report positive family and parenting relationships during reentry are less likely to recidivate. Family support services during incarceration and after release are an important strategy for increasing criminal desistance, yet family strengthening services are often a neglected aspect of rehabilitation.

There is no secret that our incarceration policies need significant policy changes at the federal, state, and local levels.

There are glimmers of hope in working for change to incarceration and release policies.

The First Step Act was passed on a bipartisan basis and signed into law in December of 2018. It deals with a number of issues including, compassionate release, changes to mandatory sentencing, how prisoners are treated including pregnant woman, with a focus on reducing recidivism. This deals only with federal prisoners but hopefully, states and local communities will follow. While this has been a big accomplishment, applauded broadly, there is much more work to be done. Hopefully, this is truly just a first step, to be followed by a second and third step to expand on these changes.

Custodial and Child Support Policies

I bring these two together because they have elements that would seem to affect each other. I was very surprised to hear that a father, who is not married to his child's mother, has limited custodial rights. In Ohio, he has virtually no custodial rights and needs to go to juvenile court to secure those rights. He may provide emotional and financial support to the mother of his child during her pregnancy, but in the eyes of the court, that does not matter. In the view of the court, you start from a near zero basis once the child is born.

So immediately you set up a potential adversarial situation, sometimes with lawyers involved, shortly after the birth of the child. A 20-something-year-old man, who has every intention of being an involved supportive father, might find himself facing court and child support costs shortly after the baby is born. Typically, he will be outgunned since a mother can often get free legal representation through a government program. A father? Not so much. Not an ideal start to being an engaged, supportive father. In speaking with the Director of the Cuyahoga County Fatherhood Initiative, he makes the comparison to a couple seeking divorce. The divorcing couple is quite often required to go to parenting class to work out the details of childcare, school pick-up and drop off and all those other details that need to be handled. With an unwed mother and father? Nothing.

Another troubling policy in some states is who gets custodial rights if something happens to the mother. Some states favor the child going to an extended family member, like an aunt or grandmother, rather than the father. And with the spike in moms going to prison in the past decades, this has become a much bigger problem.

I'm not trying to make excuses for those fathers who choose not to engage regardless of what needs to be done. But we need to give single fathers a path of least resistance to be a positive influence on their child. Many of our policies today are financial centric, but they need to be child, or even better, family centric. And even if there are resources to assist the dad in overcoming some of these barriers, educating him on what they are becomes a problem. Often a lack of education, experience, and information hinders a father from understanding what support systems are out there and what is the best course of action.

In speaking with the head of the State of Ohio's OCF (Ohio Commission on Fatherhood), and only one of three states to have a department like this, there needs to be a focus beyond the financial and on the physical, emotional, and spiritual health of the family. It appears there is only one area that gets significant funding, and that is the financial part of the equation.

We discussed earlier in this chapter the unintended adverse consequences of our welfare programs. We seem to be repeating the same mistakes in today's custodial programs and policies as we did with the War on Poverty. Failure to acknowledge our deficiencies and adjusting quickly will only lead to repeated underperformance in fixing this problem.

We need to address the shortcomings of child support issues and use it to build bridges and not drive a father away. Despite a huge effort on the part of state and local governments to improve child support programs, it isn't working. Here are some stats followed by a graph that charts our lack of progress from 1993 to 2015.

- *The number of custodial parents who were supposed to receive child support decreased from 7.3 million in 2003 to 5.8 million in 2015.*
- *The proportion of custodial parents who were supposed to receive support, but received none, increased from 24.2 percent in 1993 to 30.7 percent in 2015.*
- *While the average child support that was supposed to be received in 2015 ($5,760) was not statistically different than the average child support that was supposed to be received in 1993 ($5,786), the average amount received in 2015 ($3,447) was lower than the average amount received in 1993 ($3,778).*
- *The proportion of custodial mothers who had child support agreements increased from 59.8 percent in 1994 to 64.2 percent in 2004 but has since decreased to 52.7 percent.*
- *About $33.7 billion of child support was supposed to be received in 2015, a decrease of $14.0 billion from 2003.*

Note: Amounts for 1993 are in constant 2015 dollars.

Based on U.S. Census Bureau – Current Population Survey, 1994–2016

There needs to be a differentiation between deadbeat dads and dead-broke dads. This, from The Office of Child Support Enforcement: "In short, fathers' relationship to the child support system depended upon the perception of the reasonableness of their orders."

And reasonableness is not a static but a dynamic situation. Case in point is the big drop-off in high-paying manufacturing jobs in the '90s. What was a reasonable child support order for a father working in an automotive plant was not so reasonable when the man was laid off and could only find work in the hospitality industry.

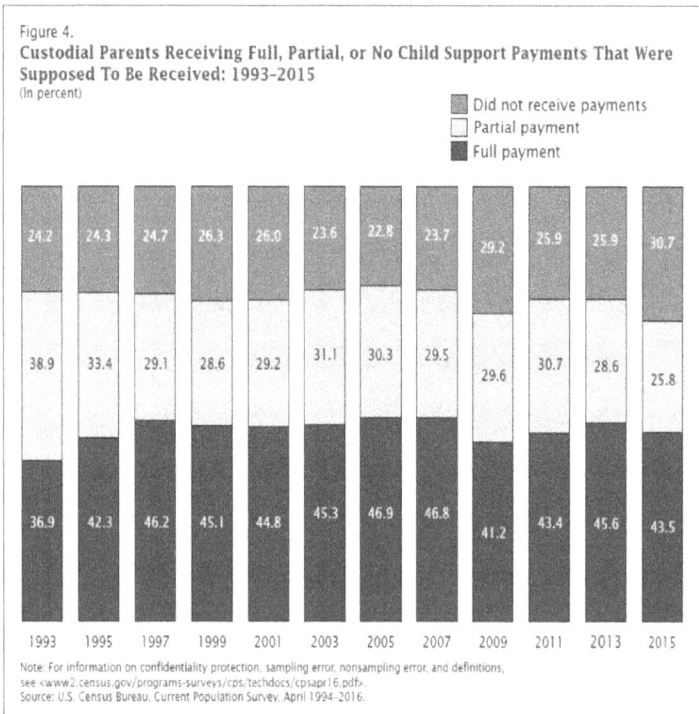

Figure 4.
Custodial Parents Receiving Full, Partial, or No Child Support Payments That Were Supposed To Be Received: 1993-2015
(In percent)

Did not receive payments
Partial payment
Full payment

Year	Did not receive payments	Partial payment	Full payment
1993	24.2	38.9	36.9
1995	24.3	33.4	42.3
1997	24.7	29.1	46.2
1999	26.3	28.6	45.1
2001	26.0	29.2	44.8
2003	23.6	31.1	45.3
2005	22.8	30.3	46.9
2007	23.7	29.5	46.8
2009	29.2	29.6	41.2
2011	25.9	30.7	43.4
2013	25.9	28.6	45.6
2015	30.7	25.8	43.5

Note: For information on confidentiality protection, sampling error, nonsampling error, and definitions, see <www2.census.gov/programs-surveys/cps/techdocs/cpsapr16.pdf>.
Source: U.S. Census Bureau, Current Population Survey, April 1994-2016.

There was a drop-off in child support collections starting in 2009. This was probably more of a factor of the economy and the recession than a case of dads choosing not to pay. The slow economic rebound in the years that followed this recession—along with stagnant wages—is no doubt a good reason why payments have not rebounded. Hopefully, with wages finally rising along with lower unemployment (pre-pandemic), we will see better results in the coming years.

Often our recourse for dads not paying is suspending drivers' licenses, jail time, fines, and penalties. These would seem to exacerbate the situation rather than helping fix the problem. If you can't drive, are in jail, or diverting monies to pay fines and penalties, the likelihood of paying your child support goes down rather than up.

To get a good in depth look at this issue, I invite you to read a book titled *Failing Our Fathers* written by Monique Jethwani, Ronald B. Mincy, and Serena Klempin.

The Cultural Shift

The last of the four major areas that appear to have contributed to the family breakdown is a shifting culture.

A number of issues have been suggested for this culture shift. Here are my findings.

- The misconception that the War on Poverty could substitute for a father's earnings power, allowing a single mom to go it alone. This false security of a woman being able to be both mother and father has been a disaster for most single moms.

- A lack of awareness and education that two heads, and in today's world, two wallets, are not only better than one when raising children but critical. Educating young males and females about the negative consequences of creating single-parent homes has got to be a priority. During my first conversation about this subject with a man who works with fathers who have been in prison, I asked why there is such a low level of conversation about this problem. His answer was an acute lack of education and awareness about the issue and its consequences. That must change. Young woman and men need to know what it will do to their health, wealth, and future standard of living along with the negative effects on their children.

- I look around and every day I see star professional athletes, those in Hollywood and others in influential roles having children before getting married. No matter how well intentioned, statistics show us that half of unmarried fathers will disappear from their child's life within five years. There are exceptions of course, but those exceptions often have the means, resources, and support structure around them that often accompany professional sports figures and other high-profile professions. Let's stop pretending that role models with means and support systems around them can be replicated by the vast majority of unmarried couples with children. They cannot. And those role models have a responsibility to acknowledge that fact.

- Our media in general, and specifically the number of sitcoms with single moms, mask the outcomes of single-parent homes. Even if things go wrong on these shows, they throw in a couple of jokes, a few laugh lines, and all turns out well. In real life, things don't often turn out well in the course of being a single mom. I saw an article titled "Television Shows That Give Single Mom Creds." I'm still scratching my head over it. While single moms do deserve an enormous amount of credit, we shouldn't marginalize the disadvantages of single moms and their children, no matter how great the desire and effort.

- For a breakdown of valuing our children, here are six items:
    - The safety situation in our cities. How many of our young children are victims of violence each week by simply being in the wrong place at the wrong time? And it just keeps getting worse. The

following is from a March 2018 *Washington Post* article by Christopher Ingraham:

At least 26,000 children and teenagers younger than 18 were killed by gunfire in the United States between 1999 and 2016, according to mortality data from the Centers for Disease Control and Prevention... Among the world's wealthy nations, the United States accounts for 91 percent of all firearm deaths of children younger than 15, according to a 2010 study published in the American Journal of Medicine... Most (15,407, or 59 percent) of the 26,000 childhood gun fatalities since 1999 are homicides. There were 8,102 childhood gun suicides over this period, 1,899 unintentional shooting fatalities and 450 shooting deaths of undetermined intent.

o   Regardless of your views on abortion, it was just incredibly callous when a law allowing abortion at nine months in New York was not only passed but celebrated. Standing ovation in the chamber when passed and then Governor Cuomo had the unimaginable callousness to light up monuments in celebration. How does anyone celebrate the potential deaths of hundreds, maybe thousands, of babies just before they are born?

- Education:
  - The subpar performance of too many school districts, city and rural, around the country has been a problem for several generations now. Pre-pandemic illiteracy around the world shrunk every day, and here in the U.S. we just turn a blind eye to this continuing problem. Structural changes and school choice need to become a reality for the many and not the few based on income or circumstance.
  - Student debt has topped a trillion dollars and everyone agrees it's a problem that will continue to grow and resonate for years. There's a lot of chatter but no real work is being done on this. Why do we not only allow, but encourage, an 18-year-old who may not know the basics of compounded debt to start off their adult life with tens of thousands of dollars of debt? What makes things worse is that many will not even finish with a degree. Student debt is now larger than credit card debt in this country. The answer isn't debt forgiveness; it's *debt avoidance*.
  - The cost of a college education is growing eight times faster than wages. How does this

happen when we have federal and state dollars being allocated to our universities and we all agree education is a key to success. Why is the economic barrier to college getting larger? Are we telling those ready for college to either forget about college or be part of the $1.4B in student debt? If education is a way of avoiding or getting out of poverty, why are we making it more painful to achieve?

- Why is education not tax deductible in most cases? Tax deductions are put into the tax code to encourage what is desirable and needed in our society. In a world of tax havens, shell companies, avoiding estate taxes, etc., you would think there would be room for education deductions.

o Child abuse in organizations like the Boys Scouts and Catholic Church. It's been decades that we have known about these problems and still not a resolution.

o The acceleration and size of our national debt. More than $25 trillion and growing. But not to worry, our leaders are kicking this can down the road, along with a host of other issues, for our children and grandchildren to deal with.

- A breakdown of fostering faith and family. I have mentioned this before but one more time, getting to the rule of seven. Our children get their moral compass from family and faith. With both breaking down, where is the focus on fostering values that will be the foundation for the next generation of achievement?

6. Conclusion

The time for self-serving bluster is over. The time for real change is here. I hope that you will be inspired to seek truth and find your role in building solutions. Both exist but are so very hard to find.

The prism I choose to look through is not racism, but how we provide opportunity and resources for the coming generations of African Americans and all races (equality, not islands) to build, grow, and prosper. I believe that education, along with safe housing, jobs, justice reform, and a return to values of family and faith are the ways to achieve this goal. If we do these things, we will take great strides toward narrowing the divide—economically and culturally.

Along with great strides in these five areas, my hope is we acknowledge the greatness of the human spirit and ability for individual achievement.

"But remember this: in the final analysis, you can believe in your dream, you can be taught, supported, motivated, and loved by others, but ultimately, your success depends on you. You must take responsibility for your body, your mind, and for your character."

Mike Schmidt

About the Author

Rick Santangelo is now semi-retired after a career in business development and consulting. His success was built on the ability to see through the haze and connect the dots of what is needed and what will make a difference.

After three years of research, conversation and study, *White Privilege or Black Disadvantage* looks through a lens that attempts to separate the real from the bluster, and connects those dots with what will matter and what will make a difference.

Nothing would please him more than for you to challenge his findings and conclusions after reading this book—and then to chart your own course of research and study. You may or may not agree with Rick, but by embarking on this challenge, you will undoubtedly expand your knowledge base and better able to make a difference. And then, we all win.

www.ingramcontent.com/pod-product-compliance
Lightning Source LLC
Chambersburg PA
CBHW022124280326
41933CB00007B/529